Photocopiable Activity Book

Year 5

Non-Fiction Writing

by Sue Garnett

Introduction

Photocopiable Non-Fiction Writing for Year 5 is designed as an aid to the busy classroom teacher planning non-fiction writing activities for the Literacy Strategy.

The author has written a selection of non-fiction example texts covering the different genres required by the Literacy Strategy. These are accompanied by Writing Frames to help children to carefully plan and carry out their own piece of writing after study of each example.

For those children who struggle to think up ideas, or who have special needs, there are writing support sheets for each activity.

The main points to remember about each different type of non-fiction writing are summarised at the beginning of each section of the book. These may be enlarged and turned into wall posters to use as a constant reminder of the points made.

Topical Resources,
P.O. Box 329,
Broughton,
Preston,
Lancashire.
PR3 5LT

Topical Resources publishes a range of Educational Materials for use in Primary Schools and Pre-School Nurseries and Playgroups.

For the latest catalogue:
Tel 01772 863158
Fax 01772 866153
e.mail:sales@topical-resources.co.uk
Visit our Website at:
www.topical-resources.co.uk

Copyright © 2002 Sue Garnett
Illustrated by John Hutchinson & Paul Sealey

Typeset by Paul Sealey Illustration & Design, 3 Wentworth Drive, Thornton, Lancashire.

Printed in Great Britain for 'Topical Resources', Publishers of Educational Materials, P.O. Box 329, Broughton, Preston, Lancashire PR3 5LT by T.Snape & Company Limited, Boltons Court, Preston Lancashire.

First Published April 2002
ISBN 1 872977 66 9

Notes for Teachers

Non-Fiction for Year 5 is designed to develop children's writing skills in non fiction. The photocopiable book contains different types of non fiction writing models and worksheets.

Aims
The book aims to improve children's writing skills by providing them with a model and then another similar idea for them to write about using a framework and following the features of that writing.

How Does it Work?
The book is divided into different types of non-fiction writing. Within each type of writing there are several models each consisting of three pages.

First Page
- This is a model of the type of writing.
- The teacher reads the model with the children.
- The teacher discusses the model looking closely at the features of it, the grammar and vocabulary used and the layout.

Second Page
- This is a work page for children who need more support, ideas and guidance. The teacher will discuss the work sheet with the children in detail and help them complete it.
- The work sheet has information about the features of that type of writing. The teacher should read it through with the children.
- The work sheet has information about how to plan the ideas and set out the piece of writing. The teacher should explain how to use it.
- This worksheet has a word bank. It gives the children ideas and correct spellings to help them with their work.
- After the children have filled it in, they will use it to help them with their final piece of work which may be in an exercise book or on a piece of paper.

Third Page
- This is a work page which most of the children in the class will use to jot down their ideas before writing a final piece of work on separate paper. The teacher will discuss the work sheet before the children use it.
- The work sheet has information about the features of that type of writing. The teacher should read it through with the children.
- The work sheet has information about how to plan the ideas and set out the piece of writing. The teacher should explain how to use it.
- After the children have filled it in, they will use it to help them write their final piece of work which may be in an exercise book or on a piece of paper.

Contents

Yr 5/6   14/1/05

• POINTS TO REMEMBER •

Instructions

- Have a title or heading
  e.g. 'How to Play'

- Have numbered lists

- Have diagrams or maps

- Usually begin with a verb
  e.g. stop; take; turn

- May have a list of things you
  need.

Town Centre
Library
Hospital

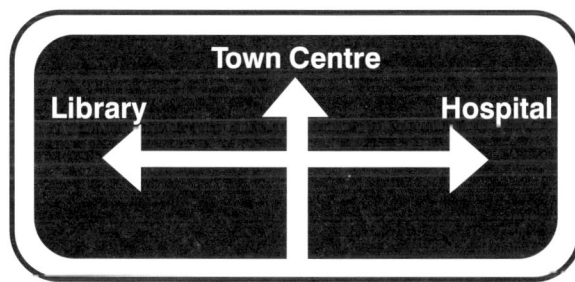

Directions to the Swimming Pool

1. From the school gate, turn left into Highfield Road.

2. Stop at the Post Office.

3. Cross over the road to the park.

4. Turn right and walk 100 metres until you reach the baker's shop.

5. Turn left by the baker's shop into Garnett Street.

6. Take the first left at Apple Trees Nursery School.

7. Go over the bridge and take the second left into Richmond Road.

8. From the end of Richmond Road, turn right into Walkman Way.

9. Follow the road until you find the swimming pool at the end.

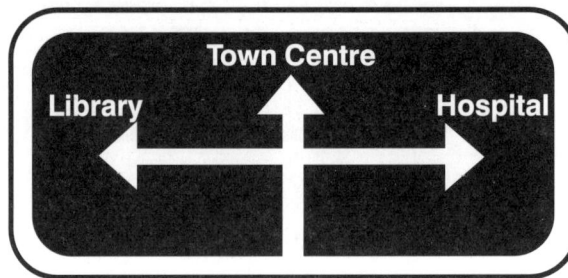

Instructions

Town Centre

Library ← ↑ → **Hospital**

Writing Support Sheet

Name: _____ **Date:** _____

Write your own instructions from school to a place of interest e.g. swimming pool, park, cinema, supermarket.

Features of Instructions

- Heading
- Numbered list
- Each instruction usually begins with a verb.
- Diagram or map

Planning Your Instructions

- Think of a place you know how to get to really well
- For each direction put a new number
- Keep your instructions short and simple.

Where from?	Where to?

Useful Ideas / Word Bank

turn

take

cross

follow

left

right

over

under

street

road

avenue

crescent

drive

park

first

second

Notes for each instruction:

1.

2.

3.

4.

5.

6.

Simple map:

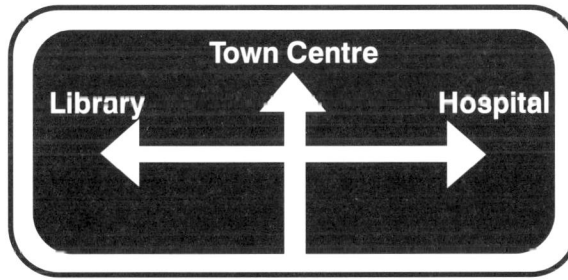

Town Centre
Library
Hospital

Name: _____ **Date:**_____

Write your own instructions from school to a place of local interest.

Features of Instructions
- Heading/title
- Numbered list
- Each instruction usually begins with a verb
- Diagram or map

Planning Your Instructions
- Think of a place you know how to get to really well
- For each direction put a new number
- Be precise with your information.

Ideas e.g. school to – swimming pool, park, cinema, supermarket etc.

Heading:

Notes for each instruction:

1.

2.

3.

4.

5.

6.

7.

Simple map:

How to Play
Scissors, Stone or Paper

Number of players: Two

Hand movements:

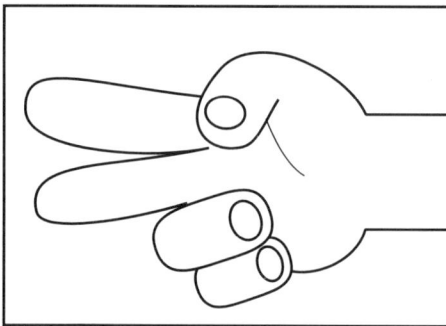

Scissors
Make a V with your forefinger and third finger.

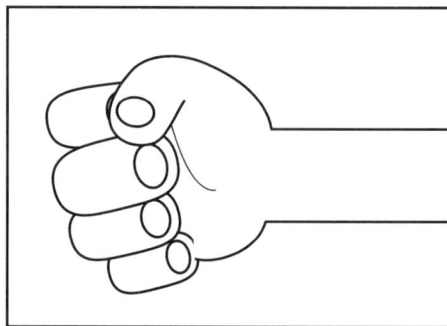

Stone
Clench your fist.

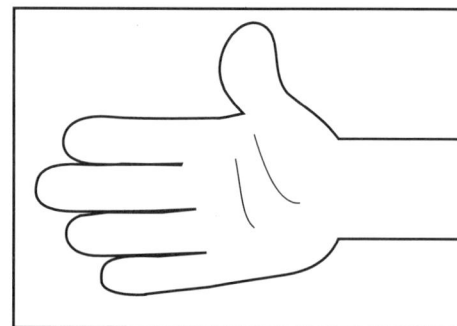

Paper
Stretch out your flat hand.

Aim:

To score points in the following way:
Scissors cut paper, so scissors scores one point.
Stone blunts scissors, so stone scores one point.
Paper wraps stone, so paper scores one point.

1   Decide how many points to win the game e.g. ten, twenty, etc.

2   On the word, "Go" each player clenches his fist and says "One, two, three – open."

3   At the word open he/she quickly makes one of the three hand movements.

4   Points will be scored according to players' hand movements.

How to Write Instructions

Writing Support Sheet

Name: _____   Date: _____

Write your own instructions for a sound or action game which doesn't need any resources.

Features of Instructions
- Heading/ Title
- Numbered list
- Begin with a doing word
- Diagram.

Planning Your Instructions
- Choose a game you know really well
  e.g. fizz/buzz, British Bulldogs, Tig etc.
- For each piece of information put a new number
- Keep the instructions clear and simple.

Title/heading:

Aim of the game:

Ideas for each instruction:

1

2.

3.

4.

5.

6.

Diagram:

Useful Ideas / Word Bank

How many people?

Aim of the game?

turns

first

second

take

next

after

score

winner

How to Write Instructions

Name: _____ **Date:** _____

Write your own instructions for a sound or action game which doesn't need any resources.

Features of Instructions	Planning Your Instructions
• Heading/ Title • Numbered list • Begin with a verb • Diagram.	• Choose a game you know really well • For each piece of information write a new number • Be precise.

Title/heading:

Aim of the game:

Ideas for each instruction:

1

2.

3.

4.

5.

6.

Diagram:

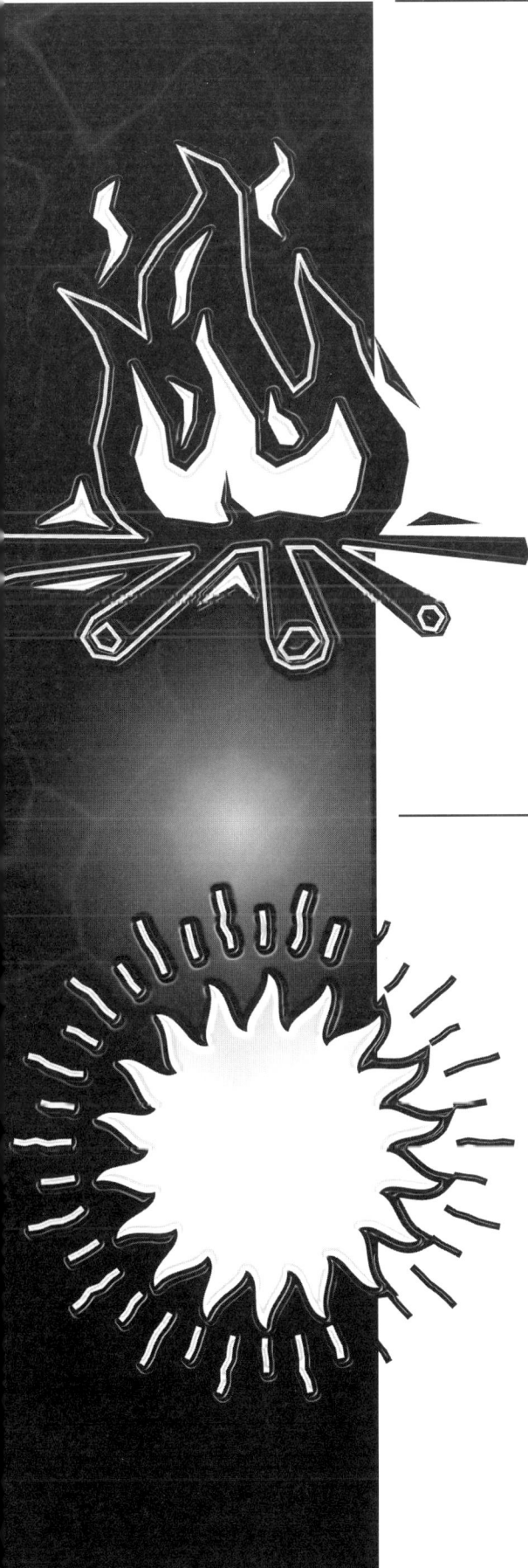

Example 3

First Aid

How to Deal With Burns

1. Put the burn under cold running water for 10 minutes.

2. If there's no water use milk or beer.

3. Take off any jewellery before the area begins to swell.

4. Dress the burn with clean non-fluffy material.

5. See a doctor if the burn is severe.

How to Deal With Sunburn

1. Take the person inside or sit them in the shade where it is cool.

2. Dip a sponge in cool water.

3. Dab the skin with the sponge.

4. Give them sips of cold water.

5. Take them to a doctor if the skin is blistered.

How to Write Instructions

Name: _____ **Date:** _____

Write your own instructions for someone needing first aid for an asthma attack or a cut.

Features of Instructions

- Heading/ Title
- Numbered list
- Begin each instruction with a doing word
- Diagram.

Planning Your Instructions

- Think of a simple injury you know how to deal with.
- Jot down the things you would need.
- Make a list of what to do.
- Sketch what happens.

Title:

What you need:

How to do it:

1.

2.

3.

4.

Diagram:

Useful Ideas / Word Bank

Asthma attack

calm

loosen clothes

inhaler

ambulance

Cut

raise

support

pressure

dressing

How to Write Instructions

Writing Frame

Name: _____ **Date:** _____

Write your own instructions for someone needing first aid e.g. asthma attack, cut, broken arm etc.

Features of Instructions
- Heading/ Title
- Numbered list
- Begin each instruction with a doing word
- Diagram.

Planning Your Instructions
- Think of first aid you know how to deal with.
- Jot down things you would need
- List exactly what to do.
- Use verbs to begin sentences.

Title/heading:

What you need:

How to do it:

1.

2.

3.

4.

5.

Diagram:

Non-Chronological Reports

- Has an introduction

- Have several paragraphs each containing different information

- Have paragraphs which may be swapped around (except for the introduction)

- May have headings and sub-headings e.g. House Martin; Song Thrush

- Contain factual information e.g. Shakespeare lived in Stratford upon Avon.

Example 1

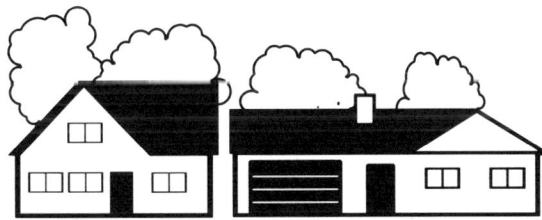

Where Birds Live

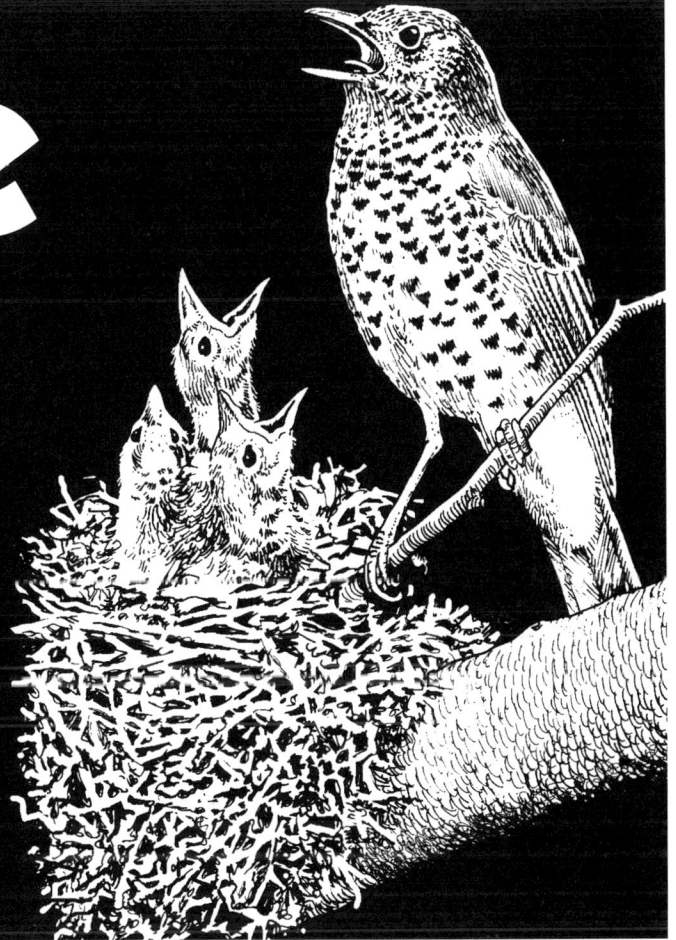

All birds (except the Cuckoo) make nests in spring and early summer. Some birds build nests in trees or bushes, others build their nests in roofs, gutters or even scrap metal objects such as an old pan.

House Martin
The house martin builds its nest under the edge of the roof of a house. It is made of little clots of mud.

Song Thrush
The song thrush builds its nest in a bush. The outer part is made of dry grass and leaves. The inner part is made of mud, rounded by the bird's body and then dried.

Magpie
The magpie builds its nest high in a tree. It is made of sticks with mud to hold them together. It has loose branches above it.

Blackbird
The blackbird makes its nest in a bush or hedge. It is made of materials such as grass, roots and broken leaves held together by mud.

Sparrow
The sparrow builds its nest under the edges of roofs or in bushes. The nests are untidy. They are made of straw, dead grass, feathers and even rubbish. Sometimes they rebuild nests from the previous season.

How to Write a Non-Chronological Report

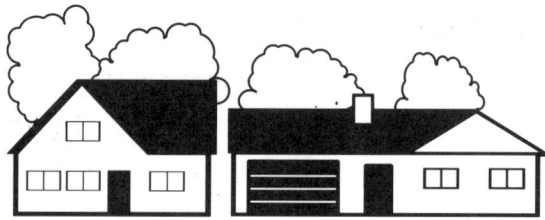

Name: _____ **Date:** _____

Write a non-chronological report about 'animal homes' or 'homes for people from around the world'.

Features of a Non-Chronological Report
- Has an introduction
- Each paragraph tells us something different
- You can swap the paragraphs around except for the introduction
- May have headings
- Often includes many facts.

Planning Your Non-Chronological Report
- Choose something you know a lot about or can find out about – you may use a non-fiction book to gather information.
- Write a general opening sentence
- Write about 3 or 4 kinds of homes.

Title:

Introduction:

Heading:
Ideas:

Heading:
Ideas:

Heading:
Ideas:

Useful Ideas / Word Bank

Animal Homes
rabbit's burrow
beaver's lodge
squirrel's drey
owl's nest
mouse hole
mole hill

tree
river
ground
soil

People's Homes
igloo
house on stilts
wigwam
mud hut
barge
flat
house

America
Lapland
Canada
Asia

How to Write a Non-Chronological Report

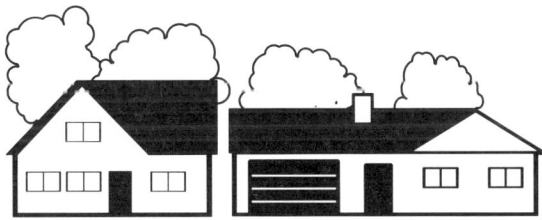

Name: _____ **Date:** _____

Write a non-chronological report about 'animal homes' or 'people's homes from around the world'.

Features of a Non-Chronological Report
- Has an introduction
- Each paragraph tells us something different
- You can swap the paragraphs around except for the introduction
- May have headings
- Contains factual information.

Planning Your Non-Chronological Report
- Choose something you know a lot about or can find out about. You may use a non-fiction book to help your research.
- Write a general opening sentence
- Write about 3 or 4 kinds of homes
- Think about – where? what? who?

Title:

Introduction:

Heading:
Ideas:

Heading:
Ideas:

Heading:
Ideas:

Heading:
Ideas:

Famous Writers

Throughout history there have been many famous writers. They have written stories, poems and plays that are still being read today.

William Shakespeare

Shakespeare wrote plays. He lived 400 years ago. He lived in the town of Stratford upon Avon. He wrote happy plays and sad plays. Two of his famous plays are 'Romeo and Juliet' which is a love story and 'A Midsummer Night's Dream' which is about magic.

William Wordsworth

Wordsworth was a poet. He lived over 300 years ago in the town of Grasmere which is in the Lake District. You can visit the house he lived in. He liked to write about the countryside. His most famous poem was called 'Daffodils'.

Charles Dickens

Dickens wrote novels. He lived in the 1800s. He wrote about how people lived in those days. Two of his famous novels are 'Oliver Twist' and 'Great Expectations'. They have both been made into films.

Agatha Christie

Agatha Christie wrote crime fiction. She is a modern writer. Two of her famous characters are 'Hercule Poirot' and 'Miss Marple'. Her books have been made into television programmes and films.

18

How to Write a Non-Chronological Report

Writing Support Sheet

Name: _____ Date: _____

Write a non-chronological report about modern authors.

Features of a Non-Chronological Report
- Has an introduction
- Each paragraph tells us something different
- You can swap the paragraphs around except for the introduction
- May have headings
- Contains factual information.

Planning Your Non-Chronological Report
- Write about something you know or can find out about
- Write a general opening sentence
- Write about 3 or 4 writers
- Give lots of factual information.

Title:

Introduction:

Heading:
Ideas:

Heading:
Ideas:

Heading:
Ideas:

Useful Ideas / Word Bank

Roald Dahl
Charlie and the Chocolate Factory

James and the Giant Peach

funny
exciting
appealing

CS Lewis
Lion, Witch and the Wardrobe

seven titles
magical
heart stopping

JK Rowling
Harry Potter
magic
popular
mysterious

How to Write a Non-Chronological Report

Writing Frame

Name: _____   **Date:** _____

Write a non-chronological report about modern authors.

Features of a Non-Chronological Report	Planning Your Non-Chronological Report
• Has an introduction • Each paragraph tells us something different • You can swap the paragraphs around except for the introduction • May have headings • Factual	• Write about something you know or can find out about • Write a general opening • Write about 3 or 4 writers • Give lots of factual information.

Title:

Introduction:

Heading:
Ideas:

Heading:
Ideas:

Heading:
Ideas:

Heading:
Ideas:

Recounts

- Are written in the past tense e.g. liked; chose; slept

- Tell the reader about something that has happened

- Have a beginning, a middle and an end.

Example 1

The Worst Day of My Life

The worst day of my life was when my dog Candy died. She was a pedigree springer spaniel and we got her when she was a pup. We chose her because she was the only one that could climb out of the basket. Dad said she had spirit. She was like a queen and used to sit on my bed all day. She never once slept in her own basket even though it was soft and warm. Candy liked to look for us through the window while we were out. She was a good dog but she didn't like the paper boy who rode a bike because he always banged on the window and teased her when he delivered the newspaper.

We had been away for the weekend to stay with relatives in Wales. We took Candy with us because she didn't like kennels. She liked going in the car and always sat with her head out of the window, her long ears flapping in the wind.

When we returned home I opened the car door and Candy shot out. She didn't usually do that but she had obviously seen something. I followed her and called her back but she carried on running. Then I saw the paper boy across the road. Candy ran straight out into the road towards him. Suddenly there was a screech of brakes and a loud bang. I ran out onto the pavement. Candy had run into a car. The driver got out of the car, his knees trembling. He said he was sorry. Candy lay still on the road. Dad picked her up and carried her inside. He said she was dead but I didn't believe him. I stroked her in my arms and even gave her the kiss of life. That was the worst day of my life.

How to Write a Recount

Writing Support Sheet

Name: _____ **Date:** _____

Write a recount about the best day or worst day of your life.

Features of Recounts
- Written in the past tense
- Tell the reader about something that has happened
- Have a beginning, middle and end.

Planning Your Recount
- Think about - What? Where? When? Who?
- Use lots of interesting words
- Write about your feelings.

Title:

What?

Who?

Where?

When?

Feelings?

Useful Ideas / Word Bank

What?
birth
death
illness
accident
celebration

Who?
Grandad/ Grandma
Friend
Brother/ Sister
Auntie/Uncle
dog,cat

Where?
road
work
school
hospital

When?
last week
last year

Feelings?
upset
delighted
helpless
sad

How to Write a Recount

Name: _____ **Date:** _____

Write a recount about the best day or worst day of your life.

Features of Recounts	**Planning your Recount**
• Written in the past tense • Tell the reader about something that has happened • Have a beginning, middle and end.	• Think about – What? Where? When? Who? • Use lots of interesting vocabulary • Write about your feelings.

Title:

What?

Who?

Where?

When?

Feelings?

Y, 5/6

1/05

The Easter Competition

Last week our school held an Easter Competition. I entered the competition (as I usually do!) There were different categories to enter. The children could choose from making an 'Easter Garden', a 'Decorated Egg' or an 'Easter Bonnet'.

I entered all three categories. Mum and I went shopping at the weekend to buy the things we'd need.

For my Easter garden I used a shallow box and filled it with soil. I put small flowers in it and made a garden fence out of lollipop sticks. For my Easter bonnet I found an old straw hat in the attic. I decorated it with paper flowers and coloured ribbon. For my decorated egg I covered a small box and painted it to look like a wall. I decorated the egg and put a face on him. I sat him on the top of the wall and wrote the title 'Humpty Dumpty'.

There were lots of entries for each category. The school cook came to judge the entries. We had a special assembly in the afternoon and the Headteacher announced the winners. There were three prizes for each category, a large Easter egg, a medium sized egg and a small egg. All the children who took part were given chocolate mini eggs.

I won second prize in the Easter garden and third prize for my Easter bonnet. The Headteacher said that it wasn't winning that was most important, but simply taking part. I couldn't wait to get home and tell my mum how I'd got on.

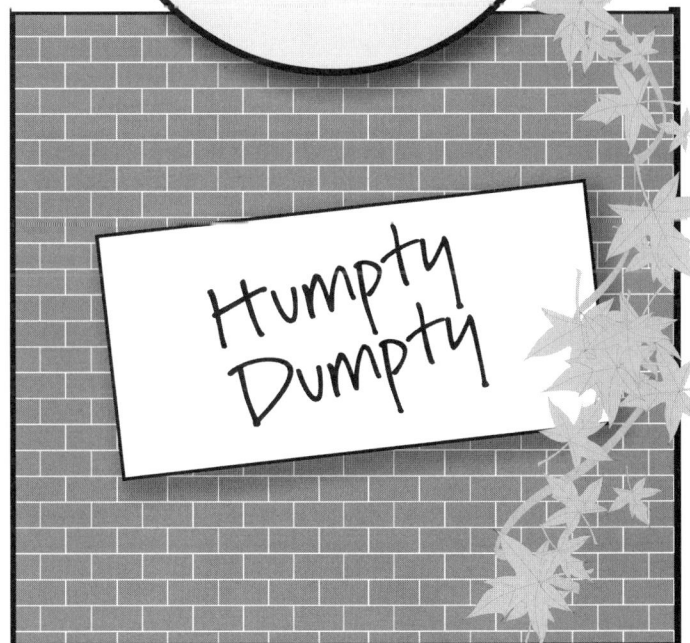

Humpty Dumpty

How to Write a Recount

Writing Support Sheet

Name: _____ **Date:** _____

Write your own recount about a special event e.g. football match, birthday party.

Features of Recounts
- Written in the past tense
- Tell the reader about something that has happened
- Have a beginning, middle and end.

Planning your Recount
- Think about – What? Where? When? Who?
- Use lots of interesting words.
- Write about your feelings.

Title:

What?

Who?

Where?

When?

Feelings?

Useful Ideas / Word Bank

What?
football match
netball match
competition
day out
party
visit somewhere

Who?
school
friends
family
brother
sister

When
last week
last month

Where?
school
house
circus
fair ground
sea side
football ground

26

How to Write a Recount

Writing Frame

Name: _____ **Date:** _____

Write your own recount about a special event e.g. sporting event, competition, day out, party etc.

Features of Recounts
- Written in the past tense
- Tell the reader about something that has happened
- Have a beginning, middle and end.

Planning your Recount
- Think about – What? Where? When? Who?
- Use lots of interesting vocabulary
- Write about your feelings

Title:

What?

Who?

Where?

When?

Feelings?

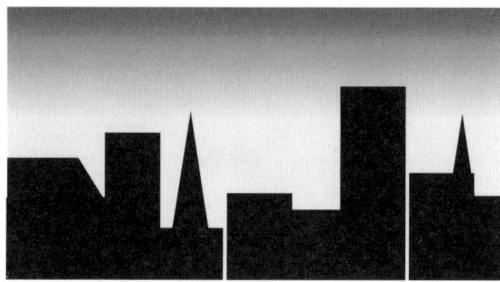

Example 3

Primary School Closes Down

On July 10th 2001 Brandwood Primary School closed its doors for the last time. The school was shut down and a brand new school was opened across the road.

The last day was very emotional. The Headteacher held an assembly in the hall. Parents and people from the local community were invited. Lots of old pupils came, some of them were in their late sixties and seventies.

One of the previous Headteachers came to the assembly. He talked about how it used to be in the early days. He talked about the outside toilets and how there were no hot dinners or any computers. He showed photographs of some of the teachers and pupils. The pictures were black and white and the children wore old fashioned clothes.

The choir sang songs and the guitar group played a few instrumentals. Two children from the top class told everyone about their time at school and all the things that they had enjoyed.

At the end of the assembly everyone sang 'Morning has Broken' followed by the school prayer. It was an emotional occasion and several of the adults cried or covered their faces.

After the special service everyone went out into the school yard. Each child set off a balloon with a message attached to it. Each message had the theme 'Hopes for the Future'. On my balloon I put 'Let there be peace'.
It was a special day and I will never forget it for as long as I live.

How to Write a Recount

Name: _____ Date: _____

Write a recount about something which happened in your town a long time ago.

Features of Recounts
- Written in the past tense
- Tell the reader about something that has happened
- Have a beginning, a middle and an end.

Planning Your Recounts
- Think about – What? Where? When? Who?
- Use lots of interesting words
- Write about feelings

	Useful Ideas / Word Bank
Title:	town
What?	accident fire flood crime e.g. murder opening
Who?	police fire engine ambulance
Where?	radio newspaper television
When?	excited happy upset worried terrified scared
Feelings?	

How to Write a Recount

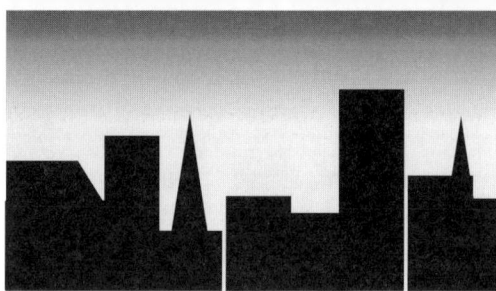

Writing Frame

Name: _____ **Date:** _____

Write your own recount about something which happened in your town a long time ago e.g. fire, flood, crime, famous event etc.

Features of Recounts	Planning Your Recounts
• Written in the past tense • Tell the reader about something that has happened • Have a beginning, a middle and an end.	• Think about – What? Where? When? Who? • Use lots of interesting vocabulary • Write about feelings.

Title:

What?

Who?

Where?

When?

Feelings?

POINTS TO REMEMBER •

Note Making

Main Teaching Points

- Only include the most important words

- The words used are mainly Nouns e.g. garden; yard; bedroom

- Words are in groups when appropriate e.g. Characters: baker, strange man, old woman

- Words are arranged in sequence e.g. setting; characters; what happened.

Example 1

A Talk About My Family

The children in class 6 were asked to give talks about their families. Gemma wrote down 'cues' to help her deliver her talk.

This is what Gemma said -
"My name is Gemma Riley and I am ten years old. I live at 22 Greenacre Gardens with my mum, dad, little brother and pet cat called Stripey.

We live in an end-terraced house with a long back yard with a garage at the side. There are three bedrooms. My room is at the back of the house and it overlooks the garden.

GEMMA RILEY — Family talk
Name
Age
Address

Family names

House — garden, yard, bedrooms, garage,
Family details- dad mechanic, mum baker,
brother nursery

My mum is thirty six years old. She works at the baker's shop in town and we get lots of free cakes. Dad is a mechanic and he works at Westwood Garage. He always comes home really dirty and smelling of oil. My little brother is called Sam. He is three years old and he goes to the nursery in the morning while mum is at work."

How to Make Notes

Name: _____ **Date:** _____

Write your own 'cues' or simple notes for a talk about your family.

Cues for a Talk Include:	Planning Your Talk
• Most important words • Mainly nouns e.g. mother, house • Words collected together in appropriate groups.	• Write headings e.g. family, house, etc to help you organise your talk • Only write words that are important otherwise you will spend too much time reading them instead of looking at the class.

Name:

Title:

Family:

House:

Jobs:

Useful Ideas / Word Bank

family
mum
dad
brother
sister
pet cat, dog

house
terraced
semi detached
detached
bungalow
flat

house
garden
yard
garage
conservatory
bedrooms

jobs
shop
factory
business

How to Make Notes

Name: _____ **Date:** _____

Write your own 'cues' for a talk about your family.

Cues for a Talk Include:
- Most important words
- Mainly nouns
- Words collected together in appropriate groups.

Planning Your Biography
- Write headings e.g. family, house, etc to help you organise your talk
- Only write words that are important otherwise you will spend too much time reading them instead of looking at the class.

Name:

Title:

Family:

House:

Jobs:

Other Facts:

Notes From a Story

The teacher read the children a story. She asked them to make notes in order that they could use them to write the whole story for their homework. This is the story the teacher told. By the side of the story are the key words Ben wrote down in his notes.

The Magic Flute

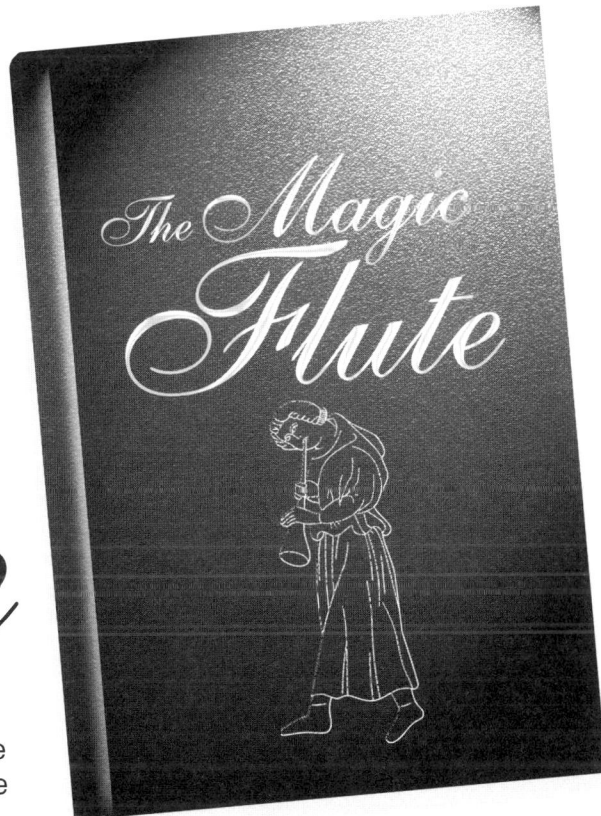

Once upon a time there was a baker who lived in a small village. One year there was a drought and the wheat growing on the farms nearby died. There was so little wheat for the baker he could only make ten loaves a day. There wasn't enough for the people in the village and soon they began to die.

One day a strange looking man came to the baker's shop and asked for some bread. There was only one loaf of bread left which the baker was going to eat himself but the old man looked so thin, the baker gave it to him.
"I'm sorry but I have no money," said the old man. "However, I can give you my flute as payment."

The baker agreed although he knew that the flute wouldn't be of much use to him.

That night the baker went outside and played the flute. Suddenly he heard a sound. He looked around and saw something beginning to grow in the field by his house. It was wheat and it was growing as if by magic. In the morning there was enough wheat to feed all the people of the village. The flute was indeed magic and the only thing the baker had to do was play to make the wheat grow. The villagers were over joyed because now they would not starve. The baker searched the village for the old man to thank him for what he had done, but the old man was never seen again.

Ben's notes – The Magic Flute.

Setting:
small village, farm

Characters:
baker, strange man

What happened:
drought, wheat died, villagers die, strange man, bread, flute, payment, played flute, wheat grew, feed villagers, not starve, baker, searched village

Ending:
man never seen again

How to Write Notes

The Dragon

Name: _____ **Date:** _____

The teacher will read you a fairy story. Make notes and then rewrite the story.

Features of Notemaking
- Most important words
- Mainly nouns
- Words arranged in order of sequence
- Words grouped when appropriate.

Planning Your Ideas
- Listen carefully to the story
- Don't try to write everything the teacher says
- Spread out your notes.

Title:

Setting:

Characters:

What Happened:

Ending:

Useful Ideas / Word Bank

long time ago

forest

castle

palace

wood/forest

witch

queen

king

giant

prince

princess

happily

How to Write Notes

Writing Frame

Name: _____ **Date:** _____

The teacher will read you a fairy story. Make notes and then rewrite the story.

Features of Note Making	Planning Your Ideas
• Most important words • Mainly nouns • Words arranged in order of sequence • Words grouped when appropriate.	• Listen carefully to what the teacher tells you • Don't try to write everything the teacher says • Spread out your notes.

Title:

Setting:

Characters:

What Happened:

Ending:

• POINTS TO REMEMBER •

Evaluations

- Use formal language
  e.g. not appropriate;
  not always accurate

- Are impersonal
  e.g. The writer could have…

- Are clear and precise
  e.g. The writer has achieved
  the intended outcome.

- Are honest.

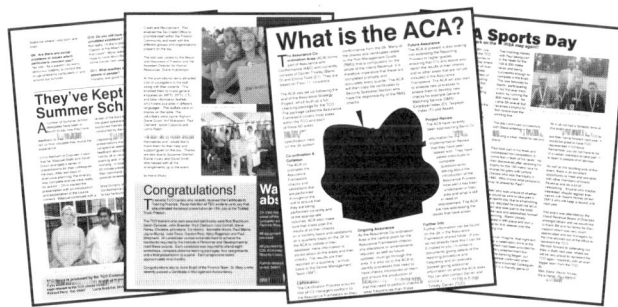

The School Newsletter

Information

The school newsletter is written every half term by a group of children from Y6. It is for families to read. It consists of four A4 pages and is in black and white print. It is written on the computer and includes pictures. The first page is a letter from the group, the second page is class news, the third page is about individual children and the fourth page is about special events.

Quality of Writing

The quality of writing is quite good. It is easy to understand and the writers use words children will understand. However, there are several spelling mistakes. The information is up-to-date and contains lots of facts. The information is interesting although it is not always accurate.

Presentation

The newsletter is presented well. The front page is bright and cheerful with a clear heading. The pictures are created on the computer and although they are well drawn sometimes they are not appropriate for the topic.

Audience Appeal

The newsletter appeals to its audience i.e. parents and children. However, the language is sometimes too difficult for younger children to read and understand.

School Bulletin
Tuesday 4th July   Issue 12

Tennis Triumph

Townly School have done it again, with a resunding victory in the under 13's Lancashire Schools Tennis Champonships

The competition is run throughout Lancashire, with all schools eligable to enter.

The later stages of the Championship had our teem up against some very stiff competition this year and Steven Patterson, the team captain admitted that the team were up against some superb players.

The trophy will be on show in the display cabinet outside the Sports hall, where it will stay until next year's competition.

It's Science Week!

The school has gone science mad!

A full week of activities that would amuse even Einstein!
Turn to page 3 for details

How to Write an Evaluation

Name: _____   **Date:** _____

Write an evaluation of a school magazine, quiz book or news-letter written by children.

Features of an Evaluation
- Uses formal language
- Is impersonal
- Is clear and precise
- Is honest.

Planning Your Evaluation
- Look at the headings
- Use adjectives to help you
- Write it in the present tense.

Title:

Information:

Quality of Writing:

Presentation:

Audience Appeal:

Useful Ideas / Word Bank

special events

news

sport

football

computers

cartoons/tv

quality of writing

clear

amusing

mistakes

spelling

presentation

pictures

photographs

colour

black and white

information

factual

interesting

How to Write an Evaluation

Writing Frame

Name: _____ **Date:** _____

Write an evaluation of a school magazine, quiz book or news-letter written by children.

Features of an Evaluation
- Uses formal language
- Is impersonal
- Is clear and precise
- Is honest.

Planning Your Evaluation
- Look at the headings and use them to guide you
- Use adjectives to help your evaluation
- Be as accurate as you can.

Title:

Information:

Quality of Writing:

Presentation:

Audience Appeal:

Example 2

Virtual REALITY

Lisa was always in trouble but she wanted a computer. Her parents promised to buy her one if she behaved and Lisa agreed, so on her tenth birthday she was given one as a present. She spent the first week of the holidays learning how to use it.

A couple of days later Lisa was in trouble with her parents again. She was sent to her bedroom and when she opened the door the computer was switched on.

There was a game on screen called Virtual Reality. Lisa didn't know that game. She sat down; angry she had been sent to her room.

"Would you like to live somewhere else?" asked the computer. Lisa replied yes, she was fed up with her parents and always being in trouble.

"Where would you like to go?"

There was a list of choices. Lisa chose the Arctic and pressed the button. WHOOSH! With an incredible force she shot into the computer and in a second she was in the Arctic. It was freezing cold. She could see a large polar bear nearby too.

"I want to go home," said Lisa her teeth chattering, wishing she'd never come.

Then she noticed her computer. It was still switched on. A face appeared.

"If you promise to behave yourself, you can go home," said the computer.

"Yes, yes," shivered Lisa. "I promise, I promise."

WHOOSH! Lisa was back in her bedroom, a pool of water on the floor. Lisa went downstairs and apologised for her bad behaviour. She'd learnt her lesson, a very important lesson!

Evaluation – Virtual Reality by Katie Moor

Objective – the children are asked to write a story about a magic computer. The writer has achieved the objective.

Plot – the story has a beginning, middle and end. It flows and makes sense. It is unusual and original. The setting could have been described in more detail. The ending could have been more exciting.

Grammar – it is written in sentences and capital letters and full stops are used appropriately. Speech marks and apostrophes are used correctly. It is written in paragraphs too.

Vocabulary/ descriptive language – the writer could have used more interesting vocabulary. The writer does not use similes and the piece of work has very few adjectives. A thesaurus could have been used to improve the story.

How to Write an Evaluation

Name: _____ **Date:** _____

Evaluate a story written by a child (it could be you).

Features of an Evaluation
- Uses formal language
- Is impersonal
- Is clear and precise
- Is honest.

Planning Your Evaluation
- Read the story carefully
- Make notes under each heading
- Write it in the present tense
- Use describing words (adjectives) to make the evaluation clearer.

Title:

Name of Writer:

Objective:

Plot:

Grammar:

Vocabulary/Descriptive Language:

Useful Ideas / Word Bank

plot

beginning

middle

end

flow

setting

characters

grammar

punctuation

capital letters

sentences

full stops

speech marks

apostrophes

vocabulary

description

adjectives

similes

How to Write an Evaluation

Name: _____ **Date:** _____

Evaluate a story written by a child (it could be you).

Features of an Evaluation	Planning Your Evaluation
• Uses formal language • Is impersonal • Is clear and precise • Is honest.	• Read the story carefully • Make some notes under each heading • Write it in the present tense • Use adjectives to make the evaluation clearer.

Title:

Name of Writer:

Objective:

Plot:

Grammar:

Vocabulary/Descriptive Language:

• POINTS TO REMEMBER •

Letters

- Have addresses at the top right-hand side

- Have the date underneath the address

- Begin with 'Dear'

- Are written in paragraphs

- End with Yours sincerely, or Yours faithfully.

Letter of Invitation

Class 9
Leamington Primary School
Parkway Crescent
Leamington
Yorks
21st March 2002

Invitation to the opening of an Italian Restaurant

Dear Parents,

I would like to invite you to the opening of Class 9's Italian Restaurant.

Class 9 have been studying Italy this term and in particular have been looking at the language and the food eaten there.

The new restaurant will be open from 12 noon until 2pm on 6th April. It will be organised by the children in Class 9. They will convert the classroom into a restaurant in typical red, white and green colours. They will play classical Italian music and for part of the time the guitar group will serenade the guests with their own live music. The food will be traditional Italian. You will see a menu listed below.
The waiters will all speak Italian and will translate the menu for you.

Menu
Pasta – with different meats and sauces
Pizza – with different toppings
Salad – various types
Ice cream – a selection of flavours
Fresh fruit – subject to availability
NB There will be no charge for the meals but donations will be gratefully accepted.
Please come along and support the children. The food will be delicious.

Yours sincerely,

John Daniels

John Daniels
(Class 9 representative)

How to Write a Letter

Name: _____ **Date:** _____

Write your own letter inviting parents and friends to an event that is happening at your school. (The event could be made up.)

Features of a Formal Letter
- Has the address at the top right hand side with the date underneath
- Begins with Dear…
- Is written in paragraphs
- Ends with Yours sincerely or Yours faithfully.

Planning Your Letter
- What is it about?
- What can you write for the introduction?
- What information will you include in each paragraph?
- How will you end the letter?

What?

Who?

When?

Why?

Useful Ideas / Word Bank

What?
fair
jumble sale
sports day
car-boot sale

Who?
class
parents
governors

When?
week
month
year
term

Why?
annual celebration
raise money
special occasion

How to Write a Letter

Writing Frame

Name: _____ **Date:** _____

Write a letter inviting parents and friends to an event that is happening at your school. (This could be made up.)

Features of a Formal Letter
- Address at the top right hand side with the date underneath
- Begin with Dear
- Written in paragraphs
- End with Yours sincerely or Yours faithfully.

Planning Your Letter
- What is it about? e.g. fair, sports day, jumble sale, car-boot sale etc.
- What can you write for the introduction?
- What information will you include in each paragraph?
- How will you end the letter?

What?

Who?

When?

Why?

Example 2

Letter of Complaint

Wentwood Primary School
Breezingham
Pinton
PP4 JSY
4th April 2002

Dear Councillor,

My class are doing a project on the environment. We have been exploring our community and looking at the things that please us and the things that don't.

There are many things in our community that please us including the traffic-free shopping centre and the new flower displays, shrubs and trees that have been planted in the main shopping street.

However, there is one thing that is upsetting us. Although we appreciate the modern art that has been erected outside the town hall, we are very upset by the vandalism and graffiti, which makes it look an eyesore. When the metal structures were erected everyone commented on how unusual and exciting they were. However, in just over a week or so, teenagers were seen climbing on the structures, bending the metal and in some cases breaking it. Since then we have seen teenagers using knives to engrave their names.

We believe that the council should do something about it. We would like to see the problem brought up at the next council meeting and ideas shared in an attempt to find a solution.

Yours sincerely,

Christopher Smith

Christopher Smith
Class 7 representative.

How to Write a Letter

Name: _____ **Date:** _____

Write a letter to your local councillor complaining about something you dislike in your community.

Features of a Formal Letter
- Has the address at the top right hand side and the date underneath.
- Begins with Dear
- Is written in paragraphs
- Ends with Yours sincerely or Yours faithfully.

Planning Your Letter
- What are you complaining about?
- Write each point in a new paragraph
- Give lots of information
- Explain how strongly you feel
- Use words like firstly, secondly.

What is the complaint?

What problems does it cause?

How does it make you feel?

What do you want done about it?

Useful Ideas / Word Bank

class

school

complain

graffiti

vandalism

burglaries

traffic

shops

rubbish

pollution

river

upset

disappointed

however

although

furthermore

How to Write a Letter

51

Name: _____ **Date:** _____

Write a letter to your local councillor complaining about something you dislike in your local community.

Features of a Formal Letter
- Address at the top right hand side with the date underneath
- Begins with Dear
- Written in paragraphs
- Ends with Yours sincerely or Yours faithfully.

Planning Your Letter
- What are you complaining about? e.g. vandalism
- Write each point in a new paragraph
- Give lots of factual information
- Explain how strongly you feel
- Use words like firstly, secondly.

What is the complaint?

What problems does it cause?

How does it make you feel?

What do you want done about it?

Example 3

Thank You Letter

St James' CE Primary School
Abbey Crescent
Waltham
5th October 2002

Dear Mr and Mrs Harris,

On behalf of Class 5 I would like to thank you for coming to our school to show us the play, 'Living in a Green World'.

We thought that the story was excellent. The costumes were very good, especially the ones showing the green world and the dead world. My favourite part was when you made the world change into a horrible scary place and you played the strange music and shone lights around the hall. I thought your dancing was excellent too.

The children in our school really care about our world now and have decided to do something about it. I am a member of the school council and every week we meet to discuss important things. Last week we held an emergency meeting to discuss some of the important issues you told us about in the play.

This is what we have decided to do:
- Collect waste paper and take it to be recycled.
- Encourage children to bring fruit for lunch and not sweets or chocolates.
- Join some environmental societies and find out more about them.
- Raise money for an environmental charity.

Perhaps you would be able to visit us when you are in the local area. We would be delighted to see you again.

Yours sincerely,
Harry Jones

How to Write a Letter

Writing Support Sheet

Name: _____ Date: _____

Write a thank you letter for a real or an imaginary event.

Features of a Formal Letter
- Has the address at the top right hand side with the date underneath
- Begins with Dear
- Is written in paragraphs
- Ends with Yours sincerely or Yours faithfully.

Planning Your Letter
- Decide what to thank someone for
- Decide what points you could write in each paragraph
- Decide what you are going to do to show your appreciation.

What are you thanking the person for?

What happened?

What did you enjoy?

How did you feel?

What are you going to do as a result of this?

Useful Ideas / Word Bank

What someone did for you;
- Performed for you - puppet show play, sang danced

- Invited you to a party

- Gave you a present

- Took you somewhere

How you will repay them;

- Invite them to something

- Give them a present

- Send them something

- Send them photographs

How to Write a Letter

Name: _____ **Date:** _____

Write a thank you letter for a real or an imaginary event.

Features of a Formal Letter	Planning Your Letter
• Address at the top right hand side with the date underneath • Begins with Dear • Is written in paragraphs • Ends with Yours sincerely or Yours faithfully.	• What could you thank someone for? • What points could you write in each paragraph? • What are you going to do to show your appreciation?

What are you thanking the person for?

What happened?

What did you enjoy?

How did you feel?

What are you going to do as a result of this?

Persuasive Writing / Points of View

- May disguise opinions to look like facts
  e.g. Probably the best dog food in the world!

- Justify a personal opinion
  e.g. I wouldn't buy anything else!

- May use numbered lists or bullet points

- Uses persuasive words
  e.g. I really believe this works!

- Uses questions for effect
  e.g. Does anyone care?

New School Dinners

Prices

Sausage & Mash	£1.20
Pizza	£1.60
Fish & Chips	£1.20
Cheese Burger	£0.85
Pies and Pasties	£0.65
Liver & Onions	£1.25
Puddings	£0.85

Leaflet Advertising Fast Food

Fast Food
The food of the future!

English

Fish and chips

Italian

Pizza and pasta

Chinese

Chow mein, rice, sweet and sour

Indian

Curry, naan bread, poppadoms

Why Fast Food?
- When you're in a hurry
- Saves cooking at home
- No shopping
- No mess in the kitchen
- No washing up

Price
- Great value
- You couldn't cook it for the price

Quality
- Guaranteed fresh food
- Provides adequate daily intake of protein, carbohydrates and minerals necessary for a healthy lifestyle.

PROBABLY THE BEST FOOD IN THE WORLD!

THE ONLY WAY TO EAT!
Tel 0161 4382945

"You can't get quicker food than 'Fast Food'!"

How to Write Persuasively

New School Dinners

Si meliora dies, ut vina, poemata reddit, scire velim,
charus pretium quotus arroget annus, scriptor abhinc
aliquos ... fui: qui decidali, hilar perfectus roturosquo
referri debet an inter villis atque novos? Excludat surgia
finis, "Est vetus atque probus, centum qui perficit annos."
Quid, qui deperit minor uno mense vel anno, inte
el toto est iunior anno." Utor permisso, caudaeque pilos
ut equinae paulatim vello unum, demo etiam unum, dum
cadat elusus ratione ruentis acervi, qui redit in fastos et
virtutem aestimat annis miraturque nihil nisi quod Libitina
vendique poema.

Prices

Sausage & Mash	£1.80
Pizza	£1.60
Fish & Chips	£1.20
Cheese Burger	£0.85
Pies and Pasties	£0.65
Liver & Onions	£1.25
Puddings	£0.85

Writing Support Sheet

Name: _____ Date: _____

Write a leaflet advertising school dinners or advertising your school

Features of Persuasive Writing
- Disguises opinions to look like facts
- Justifies a personal point of view
- Uses numbered lists or bullet points
- Uses persuasive words and phrases
- Often uses questions.

Planning Your Commentary
- Use adjectives
- Set out your ideas with big bold headings
- Spread your work out
- Use pictures
- Use different sizes of writing.

Clever title:

Adjectives (describing words):

Possible Questions:

Words which persuade/opinions which sound like facts:

Useful Ideas / Word Bank

School Dinners
- warming
- filling
- tasty
- scrumptious
- healthy
- balanced
- nutritional
- fresh
- varied

Persuasive Devices
- Probably the best…
- Only a fool…..
- Where else could you..
- The best choice…

New School Dinners

Si meliora dies, ut vina, poemata reddit, scire velim, charis pretium quotus arroget annus. scriptor abhinc annos centum qui decidit, inter perfectos veteresque referri debet an inter vilis atque novos? Excludat iurgia finis, "Est vetus atque probus, centum qui perfect annos." Quid, qui deperiit minor uno mense vel anno, inte el toto est iunior anno." Utor permisso, caudaeque pilos ut equinae paulatim vello unum, demo etiam unum, dum cadat elusus ratione ruentis acervi, qui redit in fastos et virtutem aestimat annis miraturque nihil nisi quod Libitina venditque poema.

Prices	
Sausage & Mash	£1.20
Pizza	£1.60
Fish & Chips	£1.20
Cheese Burger	£0.85
Pies and Pasties	£0.65
Liver & Onions	£1.25
Puddings	£0.85

Name: _____ **Date:** _____

Write a leaflet advertising school dinners or advertising your school.

Features of Persuasive Writing
- Disguises opinions to look like facts
- Justifies a personal point of view
- Uses numbered lists or bullet points
- Uses persuasive language
- Often uses questions.

Planning Your Commentary
- Use adjectives
- Set out your ideas with big, bold, clear headings
- Spread your work out
- Use pictures
- Use different sizes of writing.

Clever Title:

Adjectives:

Questions:

Persuasive devices/ambiguities (unclear, half truths):

Opinions which seem like facts:

Salesman's Talk

"Good morning madam, could I take two minutes of your precious time to share with you the latest cleaning spray from the Squeaky Clean Company.

'Spray and Go' is the latest scientifically proven cleaning spray for all your household objects. It's probably the best cleaning spray on the market and no one should be without one. I've been using it for twelve months and I wouldn't buy anything else.

Never again do you need separate sprays for your bathroom, furniture or windows. This spray does every job with 100% satisfaction.

All you do is shake the can, point it at the object that needs cleaning and press the nozzle. Then get a cloth and wipe it off. No need to go back to the kitchen to get another spray or walk around with a bag full of different types of spray.

Could you get it cheaper? No! It's half the price of one ordinary cleaning spray and it lasts twice as long.

You can buy it in several fragrances including Vanilla, Peach, and Natural. In addition, there's a money back guarantee if you are not 100% satisfied with this product.

Buy ten cans now and save 20% on the full price. Change your life in a split second. Squeaky Clean. You know what we mean!"

How to Write Persuasively

Writing Support Sheet

Name: _____ **Date:** _____

Write a sales talk selling something to a child e.g. CD player or a bicycle.

Features of Persuasive Writing
- Justifies a personal point of view
- Disguises opinions to look like facts
- Uses half truths, exaggerate
- Uses persuasive devices
- Often uses questions.

Planning Your Commentary
- Try to think of at least 4 facts/opinions
- Back up each one
- Think of a punchy last sentence

What you are selling?

What does it have? (facilities)

Adjectives (describing words):

Questions:

Persuasion/Opinions which seem like facts:

Useful Ideas / Word Bank

CD Player

excellent price

handy size

latest model

sturdy

different colours

stereo sound

bass and treble

extra features

head phones

_____

Bicycle

latest model

lightweight

comfortable

extra facilities

speedometer

adjustable

new seat design

How to Write Persuasively

Writing Frame

Topical Resources

Name: _____ **Date:** _____

Write a sales talk selling something to a child e.g. bicycle, CD player, scooter, pogo stick etc.

Features of Persuasive Writing
- Justifies a personal point of view
- Disguises opinions to look like facts
- Uses half truths, exaggerates
- Uses persuasive devices
- Often uses questions.

Planning Your Commentary
- Try to think of at least 4 facts/opinions
- Back up each one
- Think of a punchy last line.

What are you selling?

Features:

Adjectives:

Questions you could ask:

Persuasive devices:

Opinions which seem like facts:

Radio Commentary People With Disabilities

This is Jenny Lumton, reporting for Radio Start in Hornforth.

Our news focus for this week is people with disabilities. Are they treated equally? Do they have equal access to facilities? Does anyone care? This is what we found out.

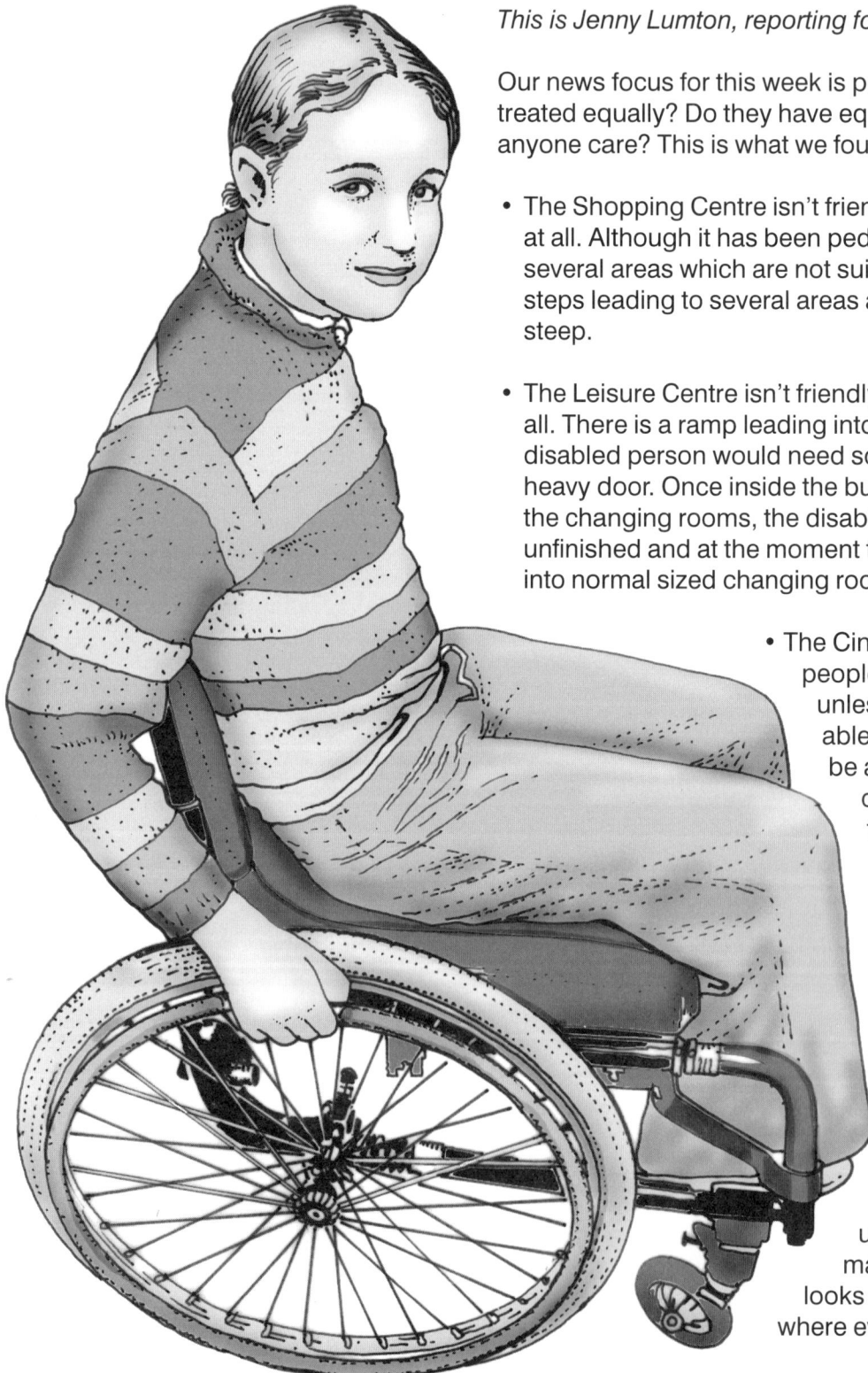

- The Shopping Centre isn't friendly for people with disabilities at all. Although it has been pedestrianised, there are still several areas which are not suitable for wheel chairs. There are steps leading to several areas and some of the ramps are too steep.

- The Leisure Centre isn't friendly for people with disabilities at all. There is a ramp leading into the building, however a disabled person would need someone with them to open the heavy door. Once inside the building, although there is a lift to the changing rooms, the disabled changing room is still unfinished and at the moment these people have to squeeze into normal sized changing rooms.

- The Cinema has a ramp and disabled people are very welcome. However, unless they are accompanied by an able bodied person, they would not be able to reach the ticket counter or refreshment stall. Once inside the cinema, for health and safety reasons, disabled people have to park their wheelchairs at the back of the cinema and sometimes are unable to sit with their friends. It's probably one of the worst cinemas in the area for disabled people.

- We have spoken to several members of the town council and they have assured us that they will look into the matter. However, until they do it looks as if we don't live in a society where everyone is treated equally.

How to Write Persuasively

Writing Support Sheet

Name: _____ Date: _____

Write a radio commentary about leisure facilities for children in your town. Focus on the weaknesses and areas in need of improvement.

Features of Persuasive Writing
- Justifies a personal point of view
- Disguises opinion to seem like fact
- Uses half truths/ exaggerates
- Uses persuasive devices
- Often uses questions.

Planning Your Commentary
- Think of 3 points you wish to discuss
- Back up each point
- Think of a punchy last comment.

Heading:

Areas of Concern:

Questions:

Words to Persuade:

Useful Ideas / Word Bank

cinema
theatre
football pitches
all weather pitches
ice rink
roller skating
swimming
parks
adventure
playground

Quality?
up-to-date
modern
old fashioned
in need of repair

Persuasive Devices
Probably the worst…
Only a fool..
Surely…

Questions
Would you..?
How can…?

How to Write Persuasively

Writing Frame

Name: _____ **Date:** _____

Write a radio commentary about leisure facilities in your town for children. Focus on the weaknesses and areas for improvement.

Features of Persuasive Writing
- Justifies a personal point of view
- Disguises opinion to seem like fact
- Uses half truths/exaggerates
- Uses persuasive devices
- Often uses questions.

Planning Your Commentary
- Think of 4 points you wish to discuss
- Back up each point
- Think of a punchy last line.

Heading:

Areas of Concern:

Questions:

Persuasive devices/unclear half truths/exaggerations: